Jeremy—
We welcome you &
love you for the joy
you bring to your
family & your friends.
Max Settle-Winick
Janet Settle
& Brad Winick

Before There Was a Before

Before There Was a Before

by

Arthur, David, and Shoshana Waskow

Illustrations by
Amnon Danziger

ADAMA BOOKS
New York

Library of Congress Cataloging in Publication Data

Waskow, Arthur I.
  Before there was a before.

  Summary: An illustrated retelling of the creation using the
words of children.
  1. Creation—Juvenile literature. [1. Creation]
I. Waskow, David, 1964—   . II. Waskow, Shoshana,
1967-   . III. Title.
BS651.W355   1983   231.7'65   84-11177
ISBN 0-915361-08-6

ADAMA BOOKS, 306 WEST 38 ST., NEW YORK, N.Y. 10018

For Paul Lichterman,
    whose memory is a blessing,
And for the people of the Floating Havurah,
    where this was written.

BEGINNING

Once upon a time there was a ------ NO! That's not the right way to start this story. This story starts even before there was any time. There were no clocks to measure the hours, and no calendars to measure the years. In fact, there weren't any hours or any years to measure. There wasn't any light, and there wasn't any dark. There wasn't any front, and there wasn't any back. There wasn't any early, and there wasn't any late.

If you want to feel what it was like then, close your eyes and look at what you see. There's a sort-of-darkness, but in the middle comes a flash of light. Then it's gone. There's a shadow of green, and then it fades away. The dark and the light are all mixed up. "Now" and "then" are all mixed up.

So that gives you the feeling of what it was like before there was a before.

But that was before there were any people, either. So whose eyes were closed?

God's eyes were closed. Pretend you're God. Pretend Your eyes are closed. Dark and light are all mixed up. "Now" and "then" are all mixed up. There isn't any world. There isn't any time. There isn't any no-time or any no-world either. There is Something, but You can't tell what it is. Everything is Everything.

Are you still pretending that you are God?

Then – You are Everything. All is God, God is All. Nothing is inside You, and

nothing is outside You. Everything is inside You, and everything is outside You. You are All Alone.

You're lonely. There's nobody to talk with. There's nothing to look at, and no one to look at You. So You're lonely, and You want company.

So You pull all of Yourself together closer, tighter, and then You separate Yourself into two parts. One part is You, and one part is empty. Open Your eyes! Now You can see the empty space. It is outside You, but there are a few sparks and streaks of You still in it. They look like shooting stars. You say "Yes!" to the emptiness and it becomes a World.

God says *Yes* again, and the World says *yes,* and they start to sing to each other "Yes – yes – yes – yes – yes!"

Each Yes takes one second to say and one second to hear, so time began.

Time began!

Once upon a time, God started feeling that this Yes – Yes – Yes was getting boring. "Let's get this world into some shape so I can have a real conversation," said God.

ONE DAY

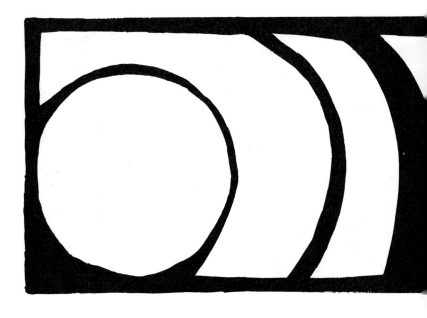

God laughed with joy to see the World lit up, and thought, "It's like a birthday. I ought to give them names!" So God called to the light, "Day!" and to the darkness God whispered, "Night." But there was no answer from either Day or Night.

God watched the light and the dark. "A twosome! That's new," said God. "I wonder, can I make two into one?" So God twirled

the dark and the light like a ball. Evening
rolled past and then morning. "Yes,
together they make one whole thing," said
God: "One Day!"

DAY TWO

T his time I'd like to listen while I look," said God, "but there's not much to hear. Day and Night had no answer for Me. The only thing the world has ever said to Me is 'Yes.' I wonder why?"

So God bent down to listen. There was plenty of noise coming from the world, but it made no sense. It sounded like *hiss, click, whoosh, buzz, hum.*

"I know the trouble," said God. "The silence and the sound are mixed with each other. It's because the World is *flowing.*"

"Hmmm?" said World.

"It's all that changing, moving, dancing, mixing stuff," said God.

"Whzzz?" said World.

So God just smiled and said, "I'll have

to show you."

Then for a while God watched and listened to the flow. "I made the World by making two; the World and Me," said God. "I made the light by making two: the light and dark," said God. "I wonder if I could make another set of *two* to clear up all this noise? I know! Let's separate two kinds of flow: waters below, rushing and streaming; heavens above, hushed and dreaming." So the World's flow divided and there was Sound below and Silence above. "Now there's a helpful set of two!" said God, and bent once more to listen.

This time the Sound was clear, and the Silence was clear. The silence picked up each sound, smoothed it out, kissed the sound, and held it gently. The silence gave each sound a shape. So now God heard the World chuckle and murmur, "Well done, Good God! Now I can talk with You in whole sentences!"

To celebrate, God gave the dark and the light another twirl. As Night's shadows fell Night whispered "Blessed be You!" and then as Day glowed forth Day called "Praised be You!"

So God called back, "Day Two!"

DAY THREE

T hen the World spoke up: "I wish I were alive like You!" But God felt puzzled. "I don't know what you mean by *alive*," God said. "I know I'm alive, but why aren't you?"

"It's because I don't know how to change myself," World said. "You keep changing by Your own Self, but I change only when You change me. If I could change myself — if I could grow and turn into something new when I wanted — then I'd be alive like You."

"That would be better," said God, "because then you'd have fresh ideas when we talked. The way it is now, I always know what you're going to say. OK, let's try," said God. "Let's see if we can make you more alive.... First of all, I don't think it

will work for the whole World to be alive. We'll need a solid place that's not alive for life to grow on. I'm My Own Place out here, but in the World your waters and your heavens are too flowing: there's no place solid. Let's pile up the changing waters, here, into this pool. I'll call this Ocean. That leaves some room for solid Land. Now life can grow on Land."

"I think You're partly right and partly wrong," said the World. "Life can grow on Ocean *or* on Land. Life can grow where things are flowing, or life can grow on some place solid. But I feel you were right to separate the Land and Ocean, anyway. I'm not sure why . . ." and the World paused to think. God waited.

"I know," said the World. "Land and

Ocean have to be separated because each one will teach its own way of living. The Ocean changes, so it will teach life how to change. The Land stands still, so it will teach life how to stay the same. And then the Ocean will teach life how to change again. Life is what grows, and stops, and then starts growing again."

World clicked. "I've got it! Can You make *seeds?*"

"You'd better explain," said God.

"I'm imagining a kind of life that starts out small and then grows bigger and changes, and then makes a tiny part of itself to start out small all over again," said World. "The tiny part could be called a *seed*. From the seed could grow roots and stems and leaves and flowers and fruit.

As the trees and grasses sprouted, their different smells spread through the World. There was the sharp smell of onion and the sweet smell of roses and the fresh smell of mint. The smells danced and turned in the air, and they woke the quiet Heavens from their drowsy dreams.

The heavens began to swirl and stir. They made no sound, but God could see the air grow thick and cloudy, then thin and clear again. The Daylight grew brighter in some places and dimmer in others. As the smells of flowers grew and spread, breezes began to blow.

The trees and grasses murmured in the wind. God heard them saying:

"How can we grow? The days are too

short for growing, the nights are too short for dying. But we have no other way to measure time."

God spoke quietly to the Heavens:

"The Earth is stirring and sprouting with life. It's the kind of life that makes me glad to smell it. I want you to have life too, but your life should take the form of light and color. As trees grow on the earth, so should lights grow in the sky.

"The trees want seasons. They need to feel the time go round like a wheel. So I want your lights to turn the seasons for the trees and grasses. I want the trees to be first cold, and then cool, and then warm, and then cold again. I want the grasses to be first dry, and then moist, and then drenched, and then dry again. I want them

to know months and years."

So the Heavens stirred and trembled, and suddenly the Daylight exploded. One ball of light burned hot and bright, and marched so slowly that it measured out a year. Another glimmered cool and pale; it swelled and thinned to make a month. And the splinters scattered into small sharp points of light.

"Sun and moon, and some stars, besides," said World. "We'll learn to live by their time. But what about the Day and Night: are they supposed to end now that the light has splintered?"

"No," said God – "I'll set the sun to rule over Day and moon to rule over Night so you will still be able to tell the difference. See – watch them set. . . and rise. . . that makes Day Four."

DAY FIVE

orld called up to God, "The trees and grasses are living and changing, but they are still not alive like You. They cannot make choices for themselves.

"They must grow where their seed falls, and they cannot move to a place they choose for themselves.

"They rustle and crackle in the wind, but they cannot choose what to speak in their own voices.

"May I ask You to shape some livelier life?"

"Yes," said God, "I want there to be life that moves and speaks. And in order to choose well where to move and what to say, this life must be able to see and hear, like Me. I have a glimmering of other

things that life will need to do, but first things first.

"I remember you said life could grow in the midst of flow; so let's start there. Let there be life that can swim in the water and life that can fly in the air. . . ."

And from all around the World rose sounds of movement: the splash of a salmon's tail against the water, the squirt of an octopus, the flapping of an eagle's wings and the hum of a bee's. And there arose also the sounds of parrots squawking and canaries trilling, lobsters clacking and whales singing.

"I am hungry to hear your voices," said God. "The trees and grasses send their smell to Me always; the sun and moon send their light to Me always; but you can

choose whether or not to send up your voices to Me.

"I am hungry to hear many many of your voices. So I want you to fill the waters and the air with moving, speaking life. Among each separate kind of you there are some males and females. Have many young, multiply, swim and fly, call to each other and to Me."

So the birds and the fish sang to God. When the sun set they began to hum in chorus, a gentle melody that dipped and curled. As night drew on the tune grew softer, a few fish carried the song through the night and then when the sun rose all the birds at once cried out their joy. Through the day they went from song to song, and as the sun dipped low again God

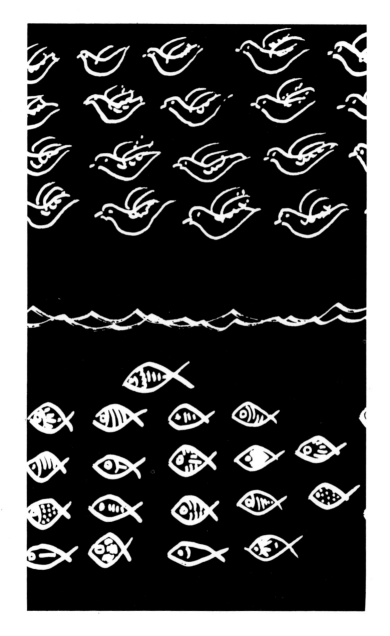

*D*arkness spread around the World. Quiet spread around the World. God watched the darkness and listened to the quiet. God murmured, "It's not enough to look, and it's not enough to listen. On the first day I looked and on the second day I listened – and then on the third day I sniffed. And on the fourth day I looked and on the fifth day I listened – so on the sixth day. . ."

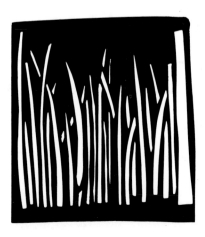

"I want to touch!" God said. "I've stayed separate from World too long; even when we talk back and forth I feel far off. I want to touch, and what's more I want the kind of life that can touch back."

From the World came a flutter of trees and grasses, waving in the dark. World smiled at God and said, "I think that life which comes from the Land itself would be touching-life. Life in the water is flowing-life, even if it touches sometimes; and life

in the air is flowing-life, even if it touches sometimes. But the Land is solid and life on the Land would *always* be touching something solid. So life on the Land would know how to touch and be touched."

"That's good," said God. "Then it's time at last for me to shape life on the Land. The birds can fly and the fish can swim, but only land animals could dance. And I love dancing!"

"Instead of shaping animals all by Yourself, you might tell the Land to give them birth," World interrupted. "Instead of just appearing on the surface they'll be held inside the earth, close touching, till they are born. Then they'll never forget how it feels to be gently touching."

"That's good," said God again. "Let the

earth give birth to animals, and let them live and grow and multiply everywhere on the Land."

The World shivered a little as lions and ants and snakes and sheep came forth and began to skip and walk and slither and creep on the Land. "They touch so much it tickles," laughed the World. "I guess we're finished now?"

"Not quite," said God. "I always work by twos. Remember? I made light and darkness, silent heavens and sounding waters, earth and ocean, trees and grasses, sun and moon, fish and birds, male and female. Today I also want to make two kinds of land animals."

World looked puzzled. "But there are thousands of land animals already. What do You mean, two?"

At first God didn't answer. World began to feel that something special was about to happen. All around the World, rabbits crept into their holes, birds settled into their nests, the wind died down, the grasses stopped rustling.

Then, with a voice that shook a little, God said: "All these animals are of one ordinary kind. Now I want to shape an animal in My Own Image."

The whole World blinked. It was almost time for the sun to rise, but the sun stopped rising. It was almost time for the birds to sing, but they sat on the edges of their nests with their big eyes wide open – silent. The crickets stopped chirping. Apples stopped falling from the trees. The waves stopped crashing onto the beach. A great hush fell across the World.

DAY SIX: THE DAWN

decide what was good to do. And once I knew, I had to decide whether to do it. So that's part of My Image too, and I want the Human to have those choices."

"Isn't that dangerous?" said the World.

"Yes," said God.

And the thunder growled across the Heavens.

God said to the sun, "I need you now. I have to be able to see very clearly." So the sun began to rise again, and the birds began to hum. The ocean waves began to roll with a low rumbling roar. The sky grew bright.

God reached out toward the World, down to the Land, and searched out a specially rich, black kind of earth. It had crushed leaves, some rotted-away bits of

tree trunk that were still warm, beetles scurrying about chewing up leaves, a crumbly-sticky feel. "That's humus," said the World. "It's great for growing things." God smiled. "I know. . .I named the Human after it, and I'm going to shape the Human from it. I want them to love each other very much."

So God began to roll and press and shape the humus until God was satisfied. Then God breathed deeply in, and out, and in again. All the winds of the World began to blow—first in stops and starts, then fiercely and wild, then gradually quieting down till they were gentle but steady. Then a soft west wind blew straight into the mouth of the shape that was lying in the mud. The chest shuddered, shook, and began to swell. Swell and go down, swell and go down.

"My breath, My wind, My spirit into your body!" said God.

"Be Human!" said God.

The Human awoke. The Human looked up at God and smiled. "Friend!" said the Human, and God smiled back.

The whole World celebrated. Goats danced on the mountaintops, and fish leaped out of the water. Brooks ran uphill, and bluebirds flew in circles. The trees turned color, from green to red and brown, and then turned back again. The moon came dancing up into the sky again, lit up in one great golden circle. God laughed and said, "That's very good!"

DAY SIX:
THE MORNING

*G*od touched the Human's arm and said, "You're thin. You need some food. It's time for breakfast anyway. I'll show you where there's food and water."

So God led the Human to a great wide garden. On every side ran streams. One was a calm, wide river, slowly slowly flowing. Another was a brook which twisted and turned through little rocks, with sudden sprays and gurgles of water. The Human giggled each time the water gurgled. Another river came racing over mountains; the Human had to look straight up to see the water falling. Still another ran like a thin thread, deep in the earth between great canyon walls.

As they came into the garden, God

turned to the Human and pointed out fruit trees and ears of corn, onion roots and walnuts. "All these are to eat," God explained, and the Human picked some almonds and some dates for breakfast.

"These," God said, "are the animals. They are yours to name and tame." Two by two, they came in a parade. Two squirrels and two wolves, two flounder and two ants, two sparrows and two ostriches, two by two they paraded past God and Human. The Human started to give them names, but suddenly stopped and turned to look at God. "Why are they all in twos?" the Human said.

God smiled. "One is male and one is female," God said. "They can have young together. And they can talk and play with each other. It's not good for them to be alone."

"How come there's only one of me, then?" said Human.

God smiled again. "There's only One of Me, and there's only one of you. That's how you're like Me. Each of us is male and female in one."

But Human frowned. "You made all this, including me?"

God nodded.

"Can I create new life, like You?"

"Not quite like Me. But the work of creation will be partly in your hands. Every time you act with love and fairness toward a tree or a sheep, that's helping make the World."

"But what love *is*, what fairness *is*,

that's what You make – not me?"

"That's right."

"And You make the way water turns to ice and how the stars burn?"

"That's right."

"Then we're *not* really like each other. I'm liable to do wrong things sometimes, and then I'll need some help."

"You can always turn to Me."

"Yes, and I'll try to, but You won't be upset and sorrowful like me. You won't have the same kind of joyfulness as me either. You're way beyond me. What I need is a counterpart, somebody like me but across from me, to be with. Why can't You remake me, to be one male and one female?"

God frowned, and the thunder

growled. "I made you this way for another reason, too. I wanted to teach all Humans that if the human race began with one person, it meant that hurting even one person is like hurting the whole human race."

The Human shrugged. "Well, that You've done already. I'll be glad to tell all future humans about it. But now I'd like there to be two of us."

God's thunder rolled much louder. "That's not My Plan!"

The Human twisted one toe nervously in the earth, liked the feel, bent down to touch the ground. "I love you, cousin," Human murmured to the humus, and then stood up again to look straight at God: "Why did you make the World?"

God hesitated, and the thunder

stopped. The sun brightened. "I was lonely," God said.

"Well, I'm lonely now," the Human answered.

God sighed. A gentle drizzle began to fall. "I guess it turns out that part of My Image is loneliness, and needing a companion. And I guess I put more of My Image in you than I thought. All right. I'll do it. Let's see. . . . It's time for your afternoon nap. Lie down."

DAY SIX:
THE
AFTERNOON

So the Human lay down. God waited while the sun grew strong and warm. The Human slowly fell into a deep, calm sleep. Then God took the two sides of the Human and separated them into one male and one female. But in separating them, God mixed a lot of female into the male and a lot of male into the female. "They're *still* a mixture," muttered God. "I'm not going to have My Image totally ruined! This way they're still both Human."

When they woke up, the male and female kissed each other. At the same moment both of them said, "We need new names now: both of us are Human . . ." They stopped and laughed, and the female said, "I'll be Woman." "Good," said the male; "I'll be Man."

But God interrupted: "That's all right, but I have something else I want to teach all future humans. From now on you, Woman, will be the one who gives birth to children. That will make it very easy for men to stop caring about children and leave all childbirth and all childcare to women. I don't want that. I want to be sure that people remember that men are really part of giving birth too, and should care about children. So maybe if I pass the word that the first Human was a Man, and that the first Man gave birth, they'll remember that men should learn to give birth. Imagine how strange the story will sound! — So they'll certainly pay attention."

Both Humans hesitated. "I'm not sure it will work that way," said Woman. "I'm older and wiser than you both!" said God, and

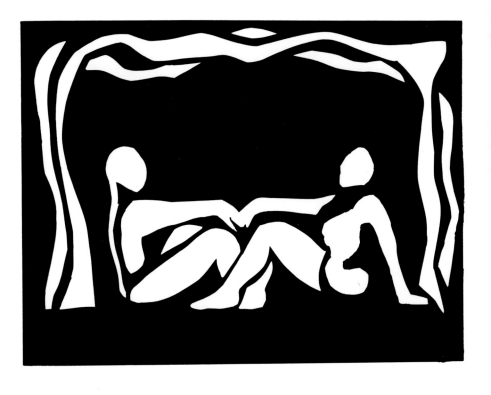

the lightning flickered. Man and Woman looked at each other and trembled. Man whispered, "I think we understand humans a little better than God does, but I'm scared. No point in arguing." Woman nodded and reached out to hold his hand. So they both said, "OK."

God smiled. "I guess that's all for now. I know you have each other but I hope you'll keep in touch with Me. Oh yes, there's this one tree – here in the center of the garden – that I don't want you to eat from. I'll explain more about that next week. But right now, I'm exhausted.

"It's been a long day today. I feel as if my own Self were partly used up. And I imagine you've had a hard day too. Is it time for sunset yet?. . . Yes. Day Six is over. Time for a rest."

"Thank God!" said Woman and Man.

RESTING

*G*od looked at the whole World and everything in it: stars and meadows, butterflies and wolves, oceans and Humans. "It was a big piece of work," God murmured. "I can feel My Self all tense and tight, concentrating so hard on the job of creation." God took a deep, deep breath and sighed a deep, deep sigh, and all of God's Self loosened and relaxed.

God said quietly to the whole World, "This is the seventh day. I make it holy. Today I will no longer make new parts of the World, and every seventh day from now on, I want all of you to live in special peace and quiet and love with each other. Today is a day for resting and singing. Today is a day for you and Me to be close in touch with each other."

"Would that include talking with You about Your teachings?" said the World, a little timidly. "Yes, of course," said God – "that's not work, that kind of study is a way of loving!"

So the World said, "I don't understand why the seventh day. Why didn't you choose to rest on the sixth or the eighth?"

The Humans had been listening, and now they joined the conversation. "Seven is a special number," they said. "We have ten fingers, and we've learned to count up to ten on them. You told us to multiply, so we learned to multiply. And we discovered that no two numbers can be multiplied to make seven, and seven can't be multiplied by anything to make any number that is ten or less. So seven isn't a *product,* and it doesn't *produce.* It's the only number up to ten that's like that. So it's the resting number."

God laughed. "That's true, but it's only one truth. There may be many other true interpretations. As for Me, I felt that My work was finished and I needed a rest. Let's dance a while. It's by dancing that I get Myself together and become a Whole."

So God began to sing to the World:
   Come, My beloved,
   Come close, My dear,
   Let's be together
   To greet the Sabbath!
And the World sang back:
   Come, true Lover,
   Come close, dear One,
   Let's be together
   To greet the Sabbath!
And together they began to dance.